ENGLAND 2022

# KIDS' HANDBOOK

WELBECK

Published in 2022 by Welbeck Children's Books Limited
An imprint of the Welbeck Publishing Group
Based in London and Sydney.
www.welbeckpublishing.com

ISBN 978-1-78312-820-4

1 3 5 7 9 10 8 6 4 2

Printed in Spain

FSC
www.fsc.org
MIX
Paper from
responsible sources
FSC® C009279

Writer: Emily Stead
Executive Editor: Suhel Ahmed
Design Manager: Matt Drew
Design: RockJaw Creative
Consultant: Anthony Hobbs

We constantly update and maintain historical records pertaining to the UEFA Women's
Championship, and additional UEFA competitions, always aiming for 100% accuracy.
Occasionally, however, new facts are brought to light, and they may have repercussions
on the accuracy here disclosed. Therefore, should you find any discrepancies in this
information, we would therefore like to offer our apologies and we would welcome your
comments.

The publisher has taken every reasonable step to ensure the accuracy of the facts
contained herein at the time of going to press, but can take no responsibility for any
incorrect information arising from changes that may take place after this point. For the
latest information, please visit: www.uefa.com/womenseuro

**The statistics and records in the book are correct as of January 2022**

The publishers would like to thank the following sources for their kind permission
to reproduce the pictures in this book.

ALAMY STOCK PHOTO: /TT News Agency: 25

GETTY IMAGES: /Aurelien Meunier/The FA: 4; /Brad Smith/ISI Photos: 16BL

UEFA: /Marc Atkins/Getty Images: 22BR; /Lars Baron/Bongarts/Getty Images: 24TR; /Shaun Botterill/Getty Images:
14; /Robert Cianflone/Getty Images: 9BL, 16BR; /Reinaldo Coddou H./Getty Images: 30L; /Thomas Eisenhuth/Getty
Images: 21BL; /Elsa/Getty Images: 18BL, 34L; /Gualter Fatia/Getty Images: 36R; /Franck Fife/AFP/Getty Images: 19BR;
/Laurence Griffiths/Getty Images: 43TR; /Alex Grimm/Getty Images: 35L; /Richard Heathcote/Getty Images: 9TR; /Maja
Hitij/Getty Images: 5, 11TR, 30R, 43BR; /Christian Kaspar-Bartke/Getty Images: 34R, 42; /Jurij Kodrun/Getty Images:
20BR, 38L, 39R; /Christof Koepsel/Getty Images: 10TR; /Daniel Kopatsch/Getty Images: 37L, 37R; /Jan Kruger/Getty
Images: 15, 31L; /Harriet Lander/Getty Images: 23BR, 26R; /Christopher Lee/Getty Images: 19BL; /Laurens Lindhout/
Soccrates: 23BL; /Charles McQuillan/Getty Images: 29L, 29R; /Damien Meyer/AFP/Getty Images: 38R; /Brendan Moran/
Sportsfile: 17BL, 17BR, 27R, 41L; /Dean Mouhtaropoulos/Getty Images: 27L, 41R, 45; /Cathrin Mueller/Getty Images:
22BL; /Jonathan Nackstrand/AFP/Getty Images: 9BR; /Oleg Nikishin/Getty Images: 36L; /Linnea Rheborg/Getty Images:
26L; /Martin Rose/Getty Images: 10-11, 12, 20BL, 28L, 33L, 33R, 46; /Alessandro Sabattini/Getty Images: 39L; /Thomas
Samson/AFP/Getty Images: 35R; /Lukas Schulze/Getty Images: 40L, 40R; /Tobias Schwarz/AFP/Getty Images: 13BR; /
Michael Steele/Getty Images: 28R; /Laszlo Szirtesi/Getty Images: 21BR, 32L, 32R; /John Thys/AFP/Getty Images: 24BL,
31R; /Jasmin Walter/Getty Images: 13L, 18BR

Every effort has been made to acknowledge correctly and contact the source and/or copyright holder of each picture any
unintentional errors or omissions will be corrected in future editions of this book.

# CONTENTS

**Note to reader: The facts and records in this book are accurate as of January 2022.**

# LONDON CALLING

With great matches being televised around the world and an evergrowing fanbase, UEFA Women's EURO 2022 is set to be an epic celebration of women's football! This handbook is your ultimate guide to the tournament, packed with facts and stats on all the teams and top players. It also includes a results chart to complete after each thrilling round. So, get reading!

## Which nations are playing?

Forty-seven nations from Europe entered the qualifying competition, with 15 teams qualifying for the final tournament alongside England, who as hosts received a bye to the finals. Northern Ireland are the only team who will be making their debut.

Hosts England hope to make a flying start in the competition.

Defending champions the Netherlands are the team to beat after claiming their first title in 2017.

## When is it happening?

After being delayed for a year due to the COVID-19 pandemic, fans are eagerly awaiting this summer's biggest football tournament – UEFA Women's EURO 2022! Manchester's Old Trafford hosts the opening match on Wednesday 6 July, marking the start of the competition which runs until Sunday 31 July.

## Where will the matches take place?

During the almost month-long festival of football, fans can watch the live matches in ten different English stadiums that span the country, from Manchester to Brighton. London's iconic Wembley Stadium will stage the final.

# ALL THE ACTION

England is hosting UEFA Women's EURO for the first time since 2005. Get to know the tournament a little better with these fast facts and brain-tickling puzzles.

## What to expect...

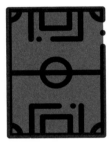
**31**
matches

**2790**
minutes of
football (at least!)

**16**
teams

**416**
players

## Hat-Trick Heroes

Meet Kai, Robyn and Ashley, the official tournament mascots! With their blend of strength, skills and smarts, they make an unstoppable trio on and off the pitch!

## Trophy Teaser

Study the shadows of the elegant EURO trophy carefully.
Circle the one that matches the trophy to the right.

A    B    C    D    E

Germany got to keep the previous trophy in 2001, after winning it three times in a row!

## Flying the Flag

Finish filling the grid with the flags of some of Europe's top teams. The puzzle should show each flag just once in each row, column and mini-grid.

1 = Germany    4 = Netherlands

2 = England    5 = Sweden

3 = France    6 = Spain

YOUR SCORE

## Shirt Scramble

Only four nations have won the UEFA Women's EURO title. Unscramble the names on the kits to work out which teams they are.

WARNYO   2

DWEENS   1

SLENDERTHAN   1

MAYNREG   8

Score an extra point if you can guess what the numbers mean!

The answers are at the back of the book.

# MY UEFA WOMEN'S EURO 2022 JOURNEY

The first of 31 epic matches kicks off on 6 July, with a capacity crowd expected at Old Trafford in Manchester! Which country will you be cheering on? Fill in your official UEFA Women's EURO 2022 profile, then make your tournament predictions.

**Name:**

**Age:**

**The country I support:**

**My favourite players:**

STICK YOUR PHOTO HERE.

**My tip to win UEFA Women's EURO 2022:**

**Best player:**

**Top scorer:**

**Best goalkeeper:**

## Lots to Spot

If you're lucky enough to be going to any of the games at England 2022, keep your eyes peeled for these matchday moments. You can join in the fun from home too, on your TV or tablet! Tick the box when you spot these eight amazing sights during the tournament.

**A goal awarded by VAR**

**A mega mascot sighting**

**A missed penalty**

**A heroic hat-trick**

**A player posing for a fan photo**

**An unfortunate own goal**

**An epic goal celebration**

**A terrific trophy lift**

# THE ROAD TO WEMBLEY

The qualifying rounds saw 15 of Europe's top teams secure their spot at UEFA Women's EURO 2022, alongside hosts England. Sides will play three group games each, before the nail-biting knockout stages begin.

## Group Stage

The first stage of the competition sees each team play three times, in a group of four. Europe's highest-ranked sides are placed in different groups. Only the top two from each group advance to the quarter-finals. Teams will try to score as many goals as possible, to boost their goal difference in case they end up tied on points.

At UEFA Women's EURO 2017, the Netherlands and Denmark met in Group A. They would meet again in the final!

## Quarter-finals

This is the first of the knockout stages. The remaining eight teams are paired up to play four ties, with the winners continuing in the competition. If the scores are level after 90 minutes, extra time is played. Penalty shoot-outs could then follow! The matches will be played in Rotherham and Wigan & Leigh in the north of England, and Brentford and Brighton in the south.

## Semi-finals

There's all to play for in the semi-finals as the four teams bid to reach the final. Ten different nations have reached the final four in previous tournaments. Sheffield and Milton Keynes will host the semi-finals this year.

## The final

London's famous Wembley Stadium is the stage for the UEFA Women's EURO 2022 final, where the remaining two teams in the competition go head to head for continental glory. Only twice has this contest been decided in extra time, with both matches won by Germany. A penalty shoot-out in the very first final saw Sweden crowned champions.

In 2017, Austria went all the way to the semi-finals in their first ever appearance at the championships.

Germany have reached the final in eight of the 12 previous editions of the tournament, winning all eight times.

# EPIC EURO FACTS

So much history has been made since the first competition was contested in 1984 to decide the women's champions of Europe! Check out these top ten tournament facts!

**1** Just four teams competed at the original tournament in 1984 – **DENMARK, ENGLAND, ITALY** and **SWEDEN**.

**2** **GERMANY** could have won **NINE TITLES\* IN A ROW** between 1989 and 2013, but for Norway's victory in 1993!

**3** The record attendance for a tournament match came at the 2013 final. **41,301 FANS** saw Germany beat Norway, a record that is set to be smashed at EURO 2022.

(Below) Germany celebrate victory over Norway in the final of Women's EURO 2013.

\*Won as West Germany in 1989

WINNERS
UEFA WOMEN'S EURO 2013
CONGRATULATIONS TO

**4** The youngest-ever player to play in the tournament was **UKRAINE'S OKSANA YAKOVYSHYN**, who was just 16 years, 5 months and 3 days when she first played at Women's EURO 2009.

**5** **DENMARK** have featured in four nail-biting penalty shoot-outs in the competition – more than any other nation!

**6** The oldest player was **FRANCE CAPTAIN SANDRINE SOUBEYRAND**, who was 39 years, 11 months and 6 days in her final match at Women's EURO 2013.

**7** Norway won Women's EURO 1993 **WITHOUT CONCEDING A GOAL**, thanks to their goalkeeper Reidun Seth and a world-class defence!

**9** **GERMANY'S INKA GRINGS** and **BIRGIT PRINZ** have scored more goals in the tournament than any other player – 10 each.

**8** In June 2021, **SWEDEN'S CAROLINE SEGER** became the most-capped European ever, after playing in her 215th international.

(Left) Sweden's Caroline Seger leads her side to a victory over Georgia in 2021.

(Below) Sarina Weigman lifts the trophy at Women's EURO 2017 as the Netherlands' head coach.

**10** No coach has won the trophy with two different nations – could **SARINA WIEGMAN** be the first, with Netherlands and England?

# STADIUM SPOTLIGHT

Ten terrific stadiums will host UEFA Women's EURO 2022, in some of England's most famous footballing cities. The showpiece final is set to be played at the iconic Wembley Stadium, London.

### Brighton & Hove
**Stadium name:** Community Stadium
**Capacity:** 30,000
**Tournament matches:** Group A, quarter-final
**Stadium fact:** A Premier League ground, which has also hosted England women's football games.

### London
**Stadium name:** Brentford Community Stadium
**Capacity:** 17,000
**Tournament matches:** Group B, quarter-final
**Stadium fact:** This west London stadium opened in 2020. Football and rugby matches are played there.

### London
**Stadium name:** Wembley Stadium
**Capacity:** 90,000
**Tournament matches:** Final
**Stadium fact:** 77,768 fans watched Germany beat England here in November 2019 – a record crowd for a 'Lionesses' fixture.

Wembley (below) hosted the men's UEFA EURO 2020 final, which Italy won on penalties.

Known as the 'Theatre of Dreams', Old Trafford is the second largest football stadium in the UK.

## Manchester

**Stadium name:** Manchester City Academy Stadium
**Capacity:** 7,000
**Tournament matches:** Group D
**Stadium fact:** The ground is located next door to the famous City of Manchester Stadium.

## Milton Keynes

**Stadium name:** Stadium MK
**Capacity:** 30,000
**Tournament matches:** Group B, semi-final
**Stadium fact:** The stadium is also used for rugby matches and as a music venue.

## Rotherham

**Stadium name:** New York Stadium
**Capacity:** 12,000
**Tournament matches:** Group D, quarter-final
**Stadium fact:** The New York Stadium has hosted sell-out crowds for England women's matches.

## Sheffield

**Stadium name:** Bramall Lane
**Capacity:** 30,000
**Tournament matches:** Group C, semi-final
**Stadium fact:** Football has been played at this historic stadium since 1862.

## Southampton

**Stadium name:** St. Mary's Stadium
**Capacity:** 32,000
**Tournament matches:** Group A
**Stadium fact:** More than 25,000 fans watched England v Wales here in a qualifier for the 2019 FIFA Women's World Cup.

## Trafford

**Stadium name:** Old Trafford
**Capacity:** 75,000
**Tournament matches:** Group A
**Stadium fact:** The tournament kicks off here, with hosts England in action.

## Wigan & Leigh

**Stadium name:** Leigh Sports Village
**Capacity:** 12,000
**Tournament matches:** Group C, quarter-final
**Stadium fact:** WSL side Manchester United Women play their home games here.

# GOALKEEPERS

From building the play at the back, to shot-stopping, catching the ball and organising the defence, these specialist players must stay focused at all times. Take a look at four of Europe's finest female keepers.

### PAULINE PEYRAUD-MAGNIN

When France's legendary keeper Sarah Bouhaddi took a break from international football in 2020, Peyraud-Magnin stepped up and helped France to a record-breaking 1091 minutes without conceding a goal. Her reliability and agility have seen Peyraud-Magnin cement her place for *Les Bleues*.

**Country:** France
**Club:** Juventus (Italian league)
**Born:** 17 March, 1992
**Caps:** 21

Well-travelled Peyraud-Magnin has played club football for top sides in France, England, Spain and Italy.

### SANDRA PAÑOS

Spain's No1 Paños is among the finest keepers in the women's game. Assured playing out from the back and a superb shot-stopper, she was named the 2020/21 UEFA Women's Champions League Goalkeeper of the Season with club side Barcelona. She has been key to Spain's rise up the rankings since making her international debut in 2011.

**Country:** Spain
**Club:** Barcelona
(Spanish league)
**Born:** 4 November, 1992
**Caps:** 46

Paños and Spain conceded a single goal during qualification for UEFA Women's EURO 2022.

## ELLIE ROEBUCK

England's Roebuck made her international debut in 2018, aged just 19. Cool under pressure, she thrives on keeping clean sheets against top teams, and isn't afraid to make herself heard on the pitch! Winning the tournament on home soil would be a dream come true for the athletic England ace.

**Country:** England
**Club:** Manchester City (English league)
**Born:** 23 September, 1999
**Caps:** 7

## SARI VAN VEENENDAAL

The experienced Van Veenendaal has been Netherlands' top keeper for a decade, helping her side to win UEFA Women's EURO 2017 and reach the FIFA Women's World Cup final in 2019. She is regarded among the world's best goalkeepers thanks to her quality in the air and outstanding one-on-one shutdowns.

**Country:** Netherlands
**Club:** PSV (Dutch league)
**Born:** 3 April, 1990
**Caps:** 83

Four matches are being hosted at Bramall Lane, Sheffield, the home of Roebuck's beloved Sheffield United FC.

Van Veenendaal has often worn the captain's armband for the 'Orange Lionesses'.

# DEFENDERS

Without a solid defence, it is unlikely that any team could become champions. Top defenders thrive on sniffing out danger and shutting down attacking moves, while pushing forward when they can. Here's a defensive quartet that oozes quality!

### LUCY BRONZE

Roving right-back Bronze loves to link defence with attack, and boasts a fine goals return for a full-back. Her vision, composure and perfectly timed tackles make her the leading 'Lioness' in England's backline too. A semi-finalist in 2017, Bronze will be keen to add to her impressive medals tally won at club level.

**Country:** England
**Club:** Manchester City
        (English league)
**Born:** 28 October, 1991
**Caps:** 82
**Goals:** 9

Don't be surprised to see Bronze on the scoresheet, she often saves her goals for big games!

### MAGDALENA ERIKSSON

The left-sided full-back makes defending look easy. She's already into double figures for international goals too, with a backheeled finish and an overhead kick among them! When the time comes for current captain Caroline Seger to pass on the armband, Eriksson would undoubtedly fill the role superbly for Sweden.

**Country:** Sweden
**Club:** Chelsea
        (English league)
**Born:** 8 September, 1993
**Caps:** 81
**Goals:** 10

Eriksson was part of the Swedish squad that won silver at the 2016 Summer Olympics.

## IRENE PAREDES

Spain captain Paredes is a talented central defender, who's playing the best football of her career. Comfortable playing out from the back, she has rarely put a foot wrong in more than 75 appearances for Spain. In qualification, Paredes helped *La Roja* to keep seven clean sheets in eight matches, conceding just once.

**Country:** Spain
**Club:** Barcelona (Spanish league)
**Born:** 4 July, 1991
**Caps:** 80
**Goals:** 9

Paredes became a mum to baby Mateo in September 2021.

## WENDIE RENARD

The rock at the heart of *Les Bleues'* defence, Renard is quite the force in women's football. At 1.87 m (6 ft 2 in), the French captain is a towering figure, and is frequently among the team's goalscorers from set pieces, possessing pace and great technique too. With more than international 125 caps, Renard is already a legend!

**Country:** France
**Club:** Lyon (French league)
**Born:** 20 July, 1990
**Caps:** 126
**Goals:** 29

Renard moved to France from the French territory Martinique at the age of 16.

# MIDFIELDERS

From the hard-working heartbeats of the team to the silky wingers, midfielders are expected to defend as well as attack. Playing at the highest level, they must excel at passing, crossing, tackling and shooting. Here are four of Europe's top midfielders.

### CAROLINE GRAHAM HANSEN

Norway's vice-captain, Graham Hansen made her international debut aged just 16. Her passing accuracy, tricky wing play and a fantastic goals-to-games ratio could see her become one of the tournament's stand-out performers. After exiting in the group stage in 2017, Graham Hansen is hoping to lead her side on a much better run this summer.

**Country:** Norway
**Club:** Barcelona
(Spanish league)
**Born:** 18 February, 1995
**Caps:** 88
**Goals:** 41

Graham Hansen could reach 100 international caps by the end of 2022.

### DELPHINE CASCARINO

Cascarino offers pace and trickery on France's right flank. Her ability to create chances will be vital to a squad that has lost experienced players since the 2019 World Cup. The attacking midfielder plays her club football for Lyon, where she has already won lots of silverware.

**Country:** France
**Club:** Lyon (French league)
**Born:** 5 February, 1997
**Caps:** 36
**Goals:** 8

Cascarino's twin sister, Estelle (a defender), has also played for France.

## DZSENIFER MAROZSÁN

Hungarian-born Marozsán is a gifted player with excellent technique. Germany are a stronger side when Marozsán is on the pitch – her goals, assists and creative play are key to the team's success. A century of international caps shows just how crucial a player she is for Germany.

**Country:** Germany
**Club:** Lyon (French league)
**Born:** 18 April, 1992
**Caps:** 109
**Goals:** 33

## ALEXIA PUTELLAS

The reigning UEFA Women's Player of the Year, Putellas is the driving force in Spain's midfield. Able to create chances for others and shoot herself, the left-footed midfielder has worked hard to reach the levels of Europe's elite players. In 2021 Putellas overtook Marta Torrejón as Spain's most-capped player.

**Country:** Spain
**Club:** Barcelona (Spanish league)
**Born:** 4 February, 1994
**Caps:** 93
**Goals:** 23

Marozsán made her debut for Germany as a teenager, in a match against Australia.

Putellas was crowned UEFA Women's Player of the Year in 2021, the first Spaniard to win the award.

# FORWARDS

Pace, touch and shooting accuracy are all-important skills for forwards hoping to fire their teams to EURO glory! Meet four free-scoring forwards who will be keen to be the top goalscorer this summer. Which player do you predict will win that prize?

### PERNILLE HARDER

A formidable forward with terrific technique and a lethal shot, Harder is regularly named among the world's best players. She has twice won the UEFA Women's Player of the Year award and has captained Denmark from the age of 23. Harder and her goals will be crucial to any Danish success this summer.

**Country:** Norway
**Club:** Chelsea (English league)
**Born:** 15 November, 1992
**Caps:** 131
**Goals:** 67

### JENNI HERMOSO

Hermoso's form over recent seasons has made her a world-class performer. Playing as a 'false 9', the striker is now Spain's all-time leading goalscorer. What's scary for Spain's opponents is that Hermoso boasts an equally enviable assists record.

**Country:** Spain
**Club:** Barcelona
(Spanish league)
**Born:** 9 May, 1990
**Caps:** 86
**Goals:** 42

In September 2021, Harder became Denmark's record scorer – male or female – with 66 goals.

Hermoso comes from a footballing family – her grandfather was a keeper for Spanish club Atlético Madrid.

## VIVIANNE MIEDEMA

Magical Miedema can strike with her left foot, right foot and her head. Her scoring record for the Netherlands is incredible. Not only is Miedema a goa machine, she is equally good at creating chances for her teammates. A special talent.

**Country:** Netherlands
**Club:** Arsenal (English league)
**Born:** 15 July, 1996
**Caps:** 104
**Goals:** 85

## ELLEN WHITE

The England No9's determination and strong work ethic are key to her scoring so many goals. Her height and ability to shake off defenders make her a predator in the box. White came close to winning the Golden Boot at the FIFA Women's World Cup in 2019 and will be desperate to win the award on home turf in England.

**Country:** England
**Club:** Manchester City (English league)
**Born:** 9 May, 1989
**Caps:** 101
**Goals:** 48

Look out for White's trademark 'goggles' goal celebration during the tournament.

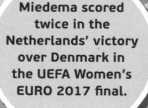

Miedema scored twice in the Netherlands' victory over Denmark in the UEFA Women's EURO 2017 final.

# FAB FINALS

Twelve fantastic UEFA Women's EURO finals have been played out so far, producing four different winners, featuring seven different finalists, plus plenty of goals! Here's how each trophy was won.

### 2017 NETHERLANDS
**Netherlands 4-2 Denmark**
**Stadium:** De Grolsch Veste, Enschede
**Attendance:** 28,182

An epic encounter between two top sides saw hosts the Netherlands score four past Denmark. Vivianne Miedema scored twice, while goals from Lieke Martens and Sherida Spitse sealed Netherlands' first-ever title.

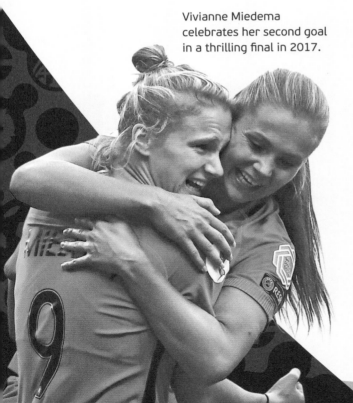

Vivianne Miedema celebrates her second goal in a thrilling final in 2017.

### 2013 SWEDEN
**Germany 1-0 Norway**
**Stadium:** Friends Arena, Solna, Sweden
**Attendance:** 41,301

Anja Mittag's solo goal in the 49th minute was enough to see Germany clinch their eighth title, while Norway had two penalties saved!

### 2009 FINLAND
**Germany 6-2 England**
**Stadium:** Olympic Stadium, Helsinki
**Attendance:** 15,877

Helsinki's Olympic Stadium staged the highest-scoring final in the competition's history. German stars Inka Grings and Birgit Prinz scored twice each, as England were overwhelmed.

Golden Boot winner Grings helps hold the trophy aloft.

### 2005 ENGLAND
**Germany 3-1 Norway**
**Stadium:** Ewood Park, Blackburn
**Attendance:** 21,105

A bumper crowd in England watched Germany secure a super sixth title. A 3-1 scoreline against a strong Norway team demonstrated Germany's dominance in Europe.

### 2001 GERMANY
**Germany 1-0 Sweden** (aet, golden goal)
**Stadium:** Donaustadion, Ulm
**Attendance:** 18,000

Germany had to wait four years to earn their fifth title (the third in a row). This time, their opponents were Sweden, and it took a golden goal from Claudia Müller to seal the victory.

## 1997 NORWAY & SWEDEN
**Germany 2-0 Italy**
**Stadium:** Ullevaal Stadion, Oslo
**Attendance:** 2,221

Germany and Italy went head-to-head, after Italy beat world champions Norway en route to the final. Germany's big-match experience paid off though, as they triumphed 2-0.

## 1995 EUROPE
**Germany 3-2 Sweden**
**Stadium:** Fritz-Walter-Stadion, Kaiserslautern
**Attendance:** 8,500

Roared on by the home crowd, Germany made it a hat-trick of titles in 1995. A 17-year-old Birgit Prinz recorded her first goal in a final (the first of five final goals she would go on to score).

## 1993 ITALY
**Norway 1-0 Italy**
**Stadium:** Stadio Dino Manuzzi, Cesena
**Attendance:** 7,000

Appearing in their fourth final in a row, Norway beat Italy to become champions for a second time. A late goal from Birthe Hegstad helped crown Norway queens of Europe once more.

## 1991 DENMARK
**Germany 3-1 Norway** (aet)
**Stadium:** Aalborg Stadion, Aalborg
**Attendance:** 6,000

*Before the 1995 tournament, matches in the women's EURO finals were only 80 minutes long.*

Germany became the first side to defend the trophy in a rematch of the previous final. This time, Germany needed extra time to beat Norway, with the winning goals coming in minutes 100 and 110!

## 1989 WEST GERMANY
**West Germany 4-1 Norway**
**Stadium:** Stadion an der Bremer Brücke, Osnabrück
**Attendance:** 22,000

West Germany, *Die Nationalelf* ("The National Eleven") scored three first-half goals from which Norway never recovered. The final finished 4-1, with the trophy changing hands to Germany.

## 1987 NORWAY
**Norway 2-1 Sweden**
**Stadium:** Ullevaal Stadion, Oslo
**Attendance:** 8,408

Sweden's hopes of defending their title were dashed when neighbours Norway scored a goal in each half to claim their first trophy, in front of a home crowd.

Sweden's Pia Sundhage scored the decisive penalty.

## 1984 EUROPE
**Sweden 1-1 England** (agg) (4-3 pens)
**Stadium:** Ullevi, Gothenburg & Kenilworth Road, Luton
**Attendance:** 5,662 & 2,567

The 1984 final remains the only championship to be decided by a penalty shoot-out. Held over two legs (with each side winning their home leg 1-0), Sweden became the first women's champions of Europe by a single penalty kick.

# Meet the Teams: Group A
# ENGLAND

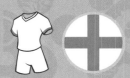

With world-beaters such as Lucy Bronze and exciting young stars including Lauren Hemp in their squad, England must soak up the pressure and make the most of their home advantage. Former Netherlands' coach Sarina Wiegman brings experience of winning a major tournament and will be aiming to win back-to-back European Championships, this time with the 'Lionesses'.

**Coach:** Sarina Wiegman
**Captain:** Steph Houghton
**Most caps:** Fara Williams (172)
**Top scorer:** Kelly Smith (46)
**Previous appearances:** 8
**Best finish:** Runners-up (1984, 2009)

Can the Lionesses roar their way to the EURO title on home soil?

## WATCH OUT FOR
Leah Williamson captained the Lionesses for the first time in 2021, and has featured at the back as well as in midfield.

# AUSTRIA

Austria finished as group runners-up behind France in qualification and will play at only their second EURO. The team surprised many by reaching the semi-finals in 2017, narrowly losing to Denmark on penalties. Equalling this finish would exceed expectations, and demand some big performances from key players such as Nicole Billa and Sarah Puntigam.

**Coach:** Irene Fuhrmann
**Captain:** Viktoria Schnaderbeck
**Most caps:** Sarah Puntigam (114)
**Top scorer:** Nina Burger (53)
**Previous appearances:** 1
**Best finish:** Semi-finals (2017)

Austria have the pedigiree to beat any of the top sides this summer.

**WATCH OUT FOR**
Goalkeeper Manuela Zinsberger is No1 for Austria and Arsenal.

# NORWAY

Having taken maximum points in qualification, Norway have the quality to go all the way to the final. Maren Mjelde, Guro Reiten and Maria Thorisdottir are three key players who all play in England, and could help secure a third European crown for "The Grasshoppers". The top teams will be wary of the threat posed by Norway this summer.

**Coach:** Martin Sjögren
**Captain:** Maren Mjelde
**Most caps:** Hege Riise (188)
**Top scorer:** Isabell Herlovsen (67)
**Previous appearances:** 11
**Best finish:** Champions (1987, 1993)

Norway scored a remarkable 34 goals in qualification and conceded just once.

### WATCH OUT FOR

Norway and Chelsea defender Maren Mjelde is one of Europe's finest full-backs.

# NORTHERN IRELAND

Northern Ireland pulled off a major shock by beating Ukraine in the play-offs to reach their first ever major tournament. Kenny Shiels' squad may enter EURO 2022 as the lowest-ranked nation, but experienced players such as Simone Magill and Rachel Furness are capable of scoring stunning goals and making more history.

**Coach:** Kenny Shiels
**Captain:** Marissa Callaghan
**Most caps:** Julie Nelson (115)
**Top scorer:** Rachel Furness (38)
**Previous appearances:** None

Northern Ireland bring a winning momentum to the tournament which will stand them in good stead.

## WATCH OUT FOR
Midfielder Rachel Furness is one of Northern Ireland's longest-serving players.

# GERMANY

Tournament winners an astounding eight times, Germany's golden girls are Europe's most successful team ever. Their squad is a mix of quality, experience and youth, boasting matchwinners in most positions. Having lost in the quarter-finals of the 2019 World Cup in France, Germany will be hungry to regain the top spot as Europe's number one team.

**Coach:** Martina Voss-Tecklenburg
**Captain:** Alexandra Popp
**Most caps:** Birgit Prinz (214)
**Top scorer:** Birgit Prinz (128)
**Previous appearances:** 10
**Best finish:** Champions (1989, 1991, 1995, 1997, 2001, 2005, 2009, 2013)

### WATCH OUT FOR

Alexandra Popp is a clever player who excels in attack as well as midfield.

Germany enjoyed a perfect qualification campaign, conceding just the one goal.

# DENMARK

Runners-up at the last Women's European Championships, the 'Red and Whites' are a well-organised side and topped their group in qualification, conceding only once. They have plenty of creative talent too – look out for captain and two-time UEFA Women's Player of the Year Pernille Harder in attack, a real matchwinner.

**Coach:** Lars Søndergaard
**Captain:** Pernille Harder
**Most caps:** Katrine Pedersen (210)
**Top scorer:** Pernille Harder (67)
**Previous appearances:** 9
**Best finish:** Runners-up (2017)

Denmark clinched qualification with a 3-1 win in Italy, who had not lost at home in more than five years.

**WATCH OUT FOR**

A scorer of important goals for Denmark, Nadia Nadim is hoping to put her injury worries behind her.

# Meet the Teams: Group B

# SPAIN

Spain's excellent progress has continued since the 2019 World Cup, earning their highest ever FIFA world ranking (10th) in 2021. La Roja ('the Red One') will bring energy and style to the competition, with Barcelona club-mates Alexia Putellas, Jenni Hermoso and Aitana Bonmatí tipped to provide the goals. Could they join Europe's elite by winning in England?

**Coach:** Jorge Vilda
**Captain:** Irene Paredes
**Most caps:** Alexia Putellas (91)
**Top scorer:** Jennifer Hermoso (42)
**Previous appearances:** 3
**Best finish:** Semi-finals (1997)

Having only ever qualified for one big final tournament before 2013, Spain are now in their fifth in a row.

**WATCH OUT FOR**
Aitana Bonmatí is one of a crop of exciting young attackers for Spain.

# FINLAND

Finland finished top of their group in qualifying, ahead of Portugal and Scotland. Nicknamed 'The Boreal Owls', their squad is made up of players who play their club football all over Europe. Women's EURO 2022 will be Finland's fourth appearance at the tournament. Their best finish – a semi-final – came back in 2005.

**Coach:** Anna Signeul
**Captain:** Tinja-Riikka Korpela
**Most caps:** Anna Westerlund (135)
**Top scorer:** Linda Sällström (49)
**Previous appearances:** 3
**Best finish:** Semi-finals (2005)

Finland claimed their qualification for Women's EURO 22 after a nail-biting late victory against Portugal.

**WATCH OUT FOR**
Finland's record goalscorer is the experienced striker Linda Sällström.

# NETHERLANDS

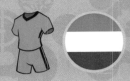

Defending champions the Netherlands are hotly tipped to reach the final in London. With superstar forward Vivianne Miedema leading the line, plus attacking-minded players who can score from almost every position, it's no surprise that the team finished as the top scorers in qualification.

**Coach:** Mark Parsons
**Captain:** Sari van Veenendaal
**Most caps:** Sherida Spitse (193)
**Top scorer:** Vivianne Miedema (85)
**Previous appearances:** 3
**Best finish:** Champions (2017)

The Netherlands will open the defence of their title with new coach Mark Parsons in charge.

## WATCH OUT FOR

Dutch winger Lieke Martens was named the official UEFA player of the tournament in 2017.

# SWEDEN

Sweden were ranked Europe's best side, and second in the world, heading into the tournament. Third at the 2019 World Cup and Olympic silver medallists, the *Blågult* ("Blue and Yellow") have a strong shot at claiming their second European title. Key players such as Magdalena Eriksson, Kosovare Asllani and teen star Hannah Bennison star for the squad.

**Coach:** Peter Gerhardsson
**Captain:** Caroline Seger
**Most caps:** Caroline Seger (223)
**Top scorer:** Lotta Schelin (88)
**Previous appearances:** 10
**Best finish:** Champions (1984)

In a clash of the titans, Sweden face title holders the Netherlands in the group phase.

**WATCH OUT FOR**
Striker Stina Blackstenius saves her best performances for big matches.

# RUSSIA

Russia are a side that are greater than the sum of their parts, being a well-organised team with a high workrate. They qualified via the play-offs, narrowly beating Portugal to secure a place in their fifth EURO finals. Yet to make it past the group stage, their challenge will be to break down the best defences in Europe.

**Coach:** Yuri Krasnozhan
**Captain:** Ksenia Tsybutovich
**Most caps:** Svetlana Petko (144)
**Top scorer:** Natalia Barbashina (46)
**Previous appearances:** 5
**Best finish:** Group stage

With seven goals, Nellie Korovkina (front row, centre) was Russia's top scorer during the qualifiers.

**WATCH OUT FOR**
Experienced defender Anna Kozhnikova has been capped more than 80 times by Russia.

# SWITZERLAND

Making only their second appearance in the competition, Switzerland booked their place after beating the Czech Republic in a dramatic penalty shoot-out. Captained by Arsenal's Lia Wälti, *La Nati* ("The Nation") will need to produce something special to reach the knockout stages. Record scorer Ana-Maria Crnogorčević and fellow striker Ramona Bachmann will need to be on form.

**Coach:** Nils Nielsen
**Captain:** Lia Wälti
**Most caps:** Martina Moser (129)
**Top scorer:** Ana-Maria Crnogorčević (61)
**Previous appearances:** 1
**Best finish:** Group stage

Switzerland's qualifying campaign included a dominant 6-0 victory over Romania.

## WATCH OUT FOR
Midfielder Lia Wälti is known for her exceptional workrate.

# FRANCE

With a stellar squad of players to choose from, including many UEFA Champions League winners, France are among the favourites in this summer's tournament. Delphine Cascarino, Marie-Antoinette Katoto and Valérie Gauvin make up a talented forward line, while Wendie Renard shores up the defence. Could Les Bleues win their first major title in 2022?

**Coach:** Corinne Diacre
**Captain:** Wendie Renard
**Most caps:** Sandrine Soubeyrand (198)
**Top scorer:** Eugenie Le Sommer (86)
**Previous appearances:** 6
**Best finish:** Quarter-finals (2009, 2013, 2017)

France's qualification campaign included an impressive 12–0 victory over Kazakhstan.

## WATCH OUT FOR

Marie-Antoinette Katoto scored 18 goals in her first 21 matches for France. Not bad!

# ITALY

While *Le Azzurre* have twice finished as tournament runners-up, they showed their best form more than 25 years ago. Today's squad, which includes top talent such as Cristiana Girelli and Barbara Bonansea, could help Italy go one better if they perform at their very best. Interestingly, almost every player in Italy's squad plays her football in the Italian league.

**Coach:** Milena Bertolini
**Captain:** Sara Gama
**Most caps:** Patrizia Panico (204)
**Top scorer:** Patrizia Panico (110)
**Previous appearances:** 11
**Best finish:** Runners-up
                 (1993, 1997)

Italy finished second in their group behind Denmark to qualify for England 2022.

**WATCH OUT FOR**

Juventus attacker Barbara Bonansea provides a real threat for Italy on the wing.

# BELGIUM

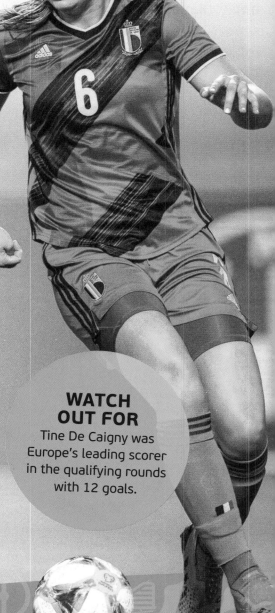

Although Belgium finished as group winners in qualification, they will be outsiders to win the competition in England. While star names such as Janice Cayman and Tine De Caigny play their football abroad, most of the squad come from the Belgian Super League. If Belgium were to make it to the knockout stages, it would be their best ever performance in a major tournament.

**Coach:** Ives Serneels
**Captain:** Tessa Wullaert
**Most caps:** Janice Cayman (117)
**Top scorer:** Tessa Wullaert (59)
**Previous appearances:** 1
**Best finish:** Group stage

Belgium put on an imperious display in a 9-0 win over Lithuania during qualification.

## WATCH OUT FOR

Tine De Caigny was Europe's leading scorer in the qualifying rounds with 12 goals.

# ICELAND

Currently ranked among the top 16 teams in the world, Iceland have every chance of making it past the group stage. This will be their fourth appearance at the finals, with their best result as quarter-finalists coming at Sweden 2013. Lyon's Sara Björk Gunnarsdóttir is a key player for the Blues, while several of the squad feature for NWSL and WSL clubs.

**Coach:** Þorsteinn Halldórsson
**Captain:** Sara Björk
        Gunnarsdóttir
**Most caps:** Sara Björk
        Gunnarsdóttir (136)
**Top scorer:** Margrét Lára Viðarsdóttir (79)
**Previous appearances:** 3
**Best finish:** Quarter-finals (2013)

Iceland finished qualifying second in their group, behind Sweden.

## WATCH OUT FOR
Midfielder Sara Björk Gunnarsdóttir is Iceland's skipper and most-capped player.

# QUIZ TIME

Can you tackle these tournament teasers in under two minutes? All the answers can be found in the book. Start the clock!

**1. Where will the first match of EURO 2022 be played?**

A. Old Trafford

B. Wembley

C. Bramall Lane

**2. Name the Netherlands No11.**

A. Sari van Veenendaal

B. Daniëlle van de Donk

C. Lieke Martens

**3. What is the nickname given to France's women's team?**

A. *Les Bleues*

B. *Les Tricolores*

C. *Le Azzurre*

**4. Which player has the most international caps of any player in Europe?**

A. Sweden's Caroline Seger

B. Netherlands' Sherida Spitse

C. Norway's Maren Mjelde

**5. Germany have won the Women's EURO the most times, but how many titles have they earned?**

A. Seven

B. Eight

C. Ten

**6. Which of these teams has never won the Women's EURO?**

A. Netherlands

B. Norway

C. England

# Golden Touch

These ten attacking players all live to score goals!
Will one of them finish as the tournament's top
scorer? Find their surnames hidden in the grid.

```
M  F  Z  X  K  T  K  R  I  B  S  N
A  S  C  F  A  O  E  K  O  L  C  Z
E  U  A  G  Y  D  S  N  E  Y  H  E
I  E  H  L  R  N  A  O  S  V  U  A
N  J  T  A  L  N  G  I  M  V  L  H
A  T  H  Y  S  S  G  I  Z  R  L  O
L  I  U  E  C  O  T  F  A  Z  E  J
L  M  A  I  Y  T  Q  R  T  C  R  H
S  A  U  K  U  O  G  Z  O  X  E  O
A  Q  L  W  S  T  Y  S  D  M  C  D
R  T  K  E  U  A  M  E  D  E  I  M
W  H  I  T  E  K  R  B  G  D  A  E
```

Tine **DE CAIGNY**
Marie-Antoinette **KATOTO**
Pernille **HARDER**
Ellen **WHITE**
Linda **SALLSTROM**
Lea **SCHULLER**

Barbara **BONANSEA**
Vivianne **MIEDEMA**
Jenni **HERMOSO**
Kosovare **ASLLANI**

# On the Ball

Here's your next challenge!
Circle which you think is the
real ball in this final battle, then
cross out the others.

The answers are at the back
of the book.

# THE GROUP STAGE

Fill in the scores after each match has been played, then complete the final group tables. The top two teams from each group progress to the quarter-finals.

| | | | | |
|---|---|---|---|---|
| 6 Jul | 20:00 | **England** ◯ v ◯ **Austria** | Trafford |
| 7 Jul | 20:00 | **Norway** ◯ v ◯ **N. Ire** | Brighton |
| 11 Jul | 17:00 | **Austria** ◯ v ◯ **N. Ire** | South'n |
| 11 Jul | 20:00 | **England** ◯ v ◯ **Norway** | South'n |
| 15 Jul | 20:00 | **Austria** ◯ v ◯ **Norway** | Brighton |
| 15 Jul | 20:00 | **N. Ire** ◯ v ◯ **England** | South'n |

| | | | | |
|---|---|---|---|---|
| 8 Jul | 17:00 | **Spain** ◯ v ◯ **Finland** | Milton Keynes |
| 8 Jul | 20:00 | **Germany** ◯ v ◯ **Denmark** | Brentford |
| 12 Jul | 17:00 | **Denmark** ◯ v ◯ **Finland** | Milton Keynes |
| 12 Jul | 20:00 | **Germany** ◯ v ◯ **Spain** | Brentford |
| 16 Jul | 20:00 | **Denmark** ◯ v ◯ **Spain** | Brentford |
| 16 Jul | 20:00 | **Finland** ◯ v ◯ **Germany** | Milton Keynes |

**Group A table**

| Team | | P | W | D | L | G | D | Pts |
|---|---|---|---|---|---|---|---|---|
| 1 | | | | | | | | |
| 2 | | | | | | | | |
| 3 | | | | | | | | |
| 4 | | | | | | | | |

**Group B table**

| Team | | P | W | D | L | G | D | Pts |
|---|---|---|---|---|---|---|---|---|
| 1 | | | | | | | | |
| 2 | | | | | | | | |
| 3 | | | | | | | | |
| 4 | | | | | | | | |

| | | | | |
|---|---|---|---|---|
| 9 Jul | 17:00 | **Russia** ◯ v ◯ **Switzerland** | W&L |
| 9 Jul | 20:00 | **Neth'ds** ◯ v ◯ **Sweden** | Sheffield |
| 13 Jul | 17:00 | **Sweden** ◯ v ◯ **Switzerland** | Sheffield |
| 13 Jul | 20:00 | **Neth'ds** ◯ v ◯ **Russia** | W&L |
| 17 Jul | 17:00 | **Sweden** ◯ v ◯ **Russia** | W&L |
| 17 Jul | 17:00 | **Switz'd** ◯ v ◯ **Netherlands** | Sheffield |

| | | | | |
|---|---|---|---|---|
| 10 Jul | 17:00 | **Belgium** ◯ v ◯ **Iceland** | Manchester |
| 10 Jul | 20:00 | **France** ◯ v ◯ **Italy** | Rotherham |
| 14 Jul | 17:00 | **Italy** ◯ v ◯ **Iceland** | Manchester |
| 14 Jul | 20:00 | **France** ◯ v ◯ **Belgium** | Rotherham |
| 18 Jul | 20:00 | **Italy** ◯ v ◯ **Belgium** | Manchester |
| 18 Jul | 20:00 | **Iceland** ◯ v ◯ **France** | Rotherham |

**Group C table**

| Team | | P | W | D | L | G | D | Pts |
|---|---|---|---|---|---|---|---|---|
| 1 | | | | | | | | |
| 2 | | | | | | | | |
| 3 | | | | | | | | |
| 4 | | | | | | | | |

**Group D table**

| Team | | P | W | D | L | G | D | Pts |
|---|---|---|---|---|---|---|---|---|
| 1 | | | | | | | | |
| 2 | | | | | | | | |
| 3 | | | | | | | | |
| 4 | | | | | | | | |

# QUARTER-FINALS

Eight teams become four in the first knockout round, the quarter-finals.

| 20 Jul | 20:00 | | v | | Brighton |
|---|---|---|---|---|---|
| Goalscorers | | | | | |

| 21 Jul | 20:00 | | v | | Brentford |
|---|---|---|---|---|---|
| Goalscorers | | | | | |

| 22 Jul | 20:00 | | v | | Wigan & Leigh |
|---|---|---|---|---|---|
| Goalscorers | | | | | |

| 23 Jul | 20:00 | | v | | Rotherham |
|---|---|---|---|---|---|
| Goalscorers | | | | | |

**Note:** All times are local times.

With 5 goals, England's Jodie Taylor was top scorer at Women's EURO 2017.

# SEMI-FINALS

Only the final four remain. Teams must win over 90 minutes or face extra time and the possibility of a penalty shoot-out in order to reach the final.

26 July,    20:00 [_____] ● v ○ [_____]                    Sheffield

Goalscorers [_____]        Goalscorers [_____]

[_____]                    [_____]

[_____]                    [_____]

Cards [_____]              Cards [_____]

Player of the match [_____]

27 July,    20:00 [_____] ● v ○ [_____]              Milton Keynes

Goalscorers [_____]        Goalscorers [_____]

[_____]                    [_____]

[_____]                    [_____]

Cards [_____]              Cards [_____]

Player of the match [_____]

**Note:** All times are local times.

> **Denmark have finished in third place a record five times.**

# FINAL

Two teams go head to head at the historic Wembley Stadium, as the final decides the champions of Europe.

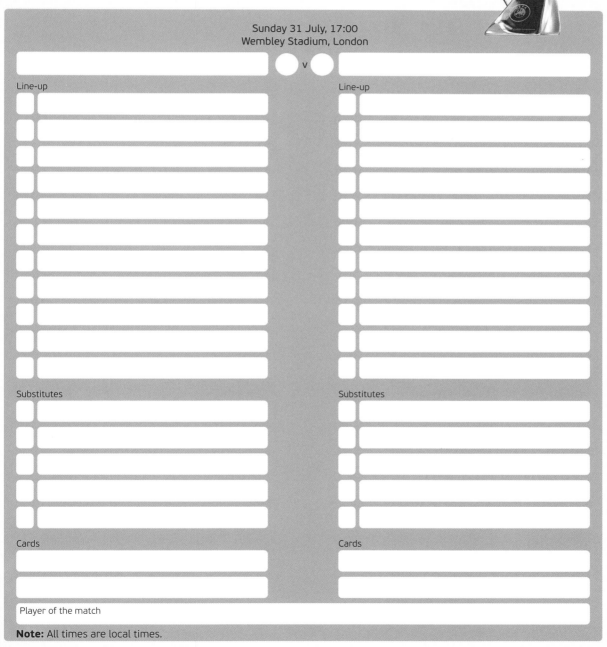

Sunday 31 July, 17:00
Wembley Stadium, London

v

Line-up

Line-up

Substitutes

Substitutes

Cards

Cards

Player of the match

**Note:** All times are local times.

# ANSWERS

## Trophy Teaser

## Flying the Flag

## Shirt Scramble

NORWAY **2**
SWEDEN **1**
NETHERLANDS **1**
GERMANY **8**

## Golden Touch

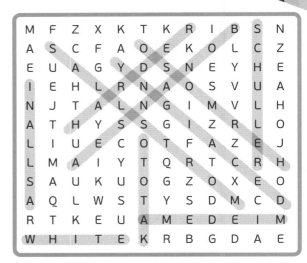

```
M F Z X K T K R I B S N
A S C F A O E K O L C Z
E U A G Y D S N E Y H E
I E H L R N A O S V U A
N J T A L N G I M V L H
A T H Y S S G I Z R L O
L I U E C O T F A Z E J
M A I Y T Q R T C R H
S A U K U O G Z O X E O
A Q L W S T Y S D M C D
R T K E U A M E D E I M
W H I T E K R B G D A E
```

## On The Ball

## Quiz Time

1. A
2. C
3. A
4. A
5. B
6. C